EARSPLITTING

Aled Turner is a North Walian writer and graduate of Kingston University's MFA Creative Writing programme. His work has been featured in *Abridged*, *Prototype*, and *Maudlin House* amongst other publications. He was recently shortlisted for the Desperate Literature prize for short fiction.

ISBN: 978-1-916938-85-4

Cover designed by Aaron Kent

Edited and Typeset by Aaron Kent

Broken Sleep Books Ltd
PO BOX 102
Llandysul
SA44 9BG

CONTENTS

Earsplitting

Aled Turner

Broken Sleep Books

PSYCHOTHERAPY

The noise sat stilly
on my tongue tip in silence
waiting to onslaught.

HOW TO KILL A CONSCIENCE

Tease guilt to the salt, a pang of boiling
Water, round penance in rubber bands
So as to avoid the nips of attrition.
Is there a humane way to kill remorse?
Hurtle the tip of a sharpened knife
Right between the eyes of contempt, score
Through the exuvia of a ripened fib,
Uproot and dispose of the tomalley in ways
Deemed fit. Twist and break with the chelae-
Once prone to seize anguish, battle affliction,
Now still in the palms of a connoisseur.
To deter recurrence, carefully scoop out
The delicacies, bite at a sac of nostalgia
And segment it between your teeth,
Forage for dregs of tact on the ribs.
Recoil any small bits of shard,
Line the mind with that of hardened
Shell, a carapace fit for a saint.

TRYST

Dead, behind the eyes an unfed mill
      of no lakes no rivers a taille a tongue
tip stiff wet against an upper lip
      stained glass, the heist of a low spring
cleaned with your mouth, a pulsating
      neck tied to an assembly of bruised
doubts at my hard thighs a song
      of something lost count air born slow
salt slewing past a chin midst
      the throes of raw myoclonus aching.

REALITY CHECK

I caught the thing in
my teeth the thing they
tried to catch in nets,
rods as long as cars
and it was a complete
and utter coincidence
the catching
or so they think as
things find their way to
my teeth periodically,
people watch
amidst rented trucks
and hand-me-down
trappings
and I chew things
before them until
the sapience
drips down my chin.

DEFINITION OF YKWTFGO

Acronym.

Phrase. (Internet slang, vulgar)

Initialism of **You know what the fuck [is] going on.**

Commonly used in an exciting manner when one is vaunting, or gassing somebody up, similarly to the exclamation, *duh* – a disdainful indication that something is obvious.

The phrase can typically be used to imply that a politician and/ or their acquaintances are in-the-know of a particular scandal, a blatant flouting of their own parliamentary rules – irrespective of any covid restrictions – a casual disregard of lawful conventions in favour of nonchalant moral failings and/or the fact that they as a government could not care less about peasantries as long as their own social gathering will be lit on the hush.

Example -

Tory 1:   We are having an incubation disco at our weekend abode – bring Sauvignon, a gram of weed and a truckle of cheese, preferably white stilton for the charcuterie.

Tory 2:   How delightful, at the expense of NHS workers?

Tory 1:   Duh. YKWTFGO.

STAIN

I'd been with Joseph
for seven years
before
he'd started wearing
protective gowns,
safety goggles,
chemical spill
boots those years
nimble fingered
interims
that sank teeth in
to my fat-
uity, both a spry,
fleet
footed execution
of my ignorance
by absorbing
candour
in towelettes,
depositing mere over
sights into biohazard
bags zip tied
with non
porous disposable
gloves
then left out
cold to dry and saw
the back

of. *With*
I shall keep
as a supple juncture,
loose-limbed a tight
lipped preposition-
some would say
in the company
of, or in addition to
the neighbour
fucking
Joseph whilst I stood
wetting down.

PIROUETTE

There, haemorrhaging a black mass
We lay raw upon a motel bed–
Listless, two cuts of chateaubriand
With cigarettes numbing at our lips.
Ash hilled upon an open torso,
Warm beer ingurgitating duvet.
Double-visioned delineations,
Blind to our blood-soaked debauchery,
A skirting board of low-wattage bulbs
That bat in room temperature; thickset
Perspiration gathered at our brows,
Ploughing copsewood as a tsunami,
Trickling past our lids, salty ions
We wipe in squint with a bare knuckle.
Look, i whisper, a palm as a psalm-
Spinning the glock in a briny hand,
The muzzle pirouetting in slow
Arced pivots, a standing ovation
With bouquets stuck to our moist shins,
Posies that marinate fatuity.
Impressive, you say, smoke rings coiling
Towards a ceiling, cold eyes that toil
In blue lights gawping a windowsill.

RESONANCE

Do you hear   how quiet
it is?   No-
You don't.   You can't.
Tranquil   ity is for
ever spoilt   by an ambient
chirr, some   thing air
bourne-   with wings-
with teeth-   yes, harm
onious, but   not with
out fault-   a mosq
uito like   crack
le- not   entire
ly still-   but nigh-
a bomb-   ilation-
a post   erior art
ery blood   flow-
plough   ing through
the aur   icular, or tin
nitus, yes.   Tin-nit-us
or tin   ni-tus.
a ring   ing
ing   ing
ing   a gut
toral churn   ing sat
at the foot   of an an-
echoic cub   icle wait
ing patient   ly to con
sume what's   left of us.

15

RICH KIDS

They gather round, the kids – knocking
out their fish,
a Mahi-Mahi.
The Poissonnier shank, scythe, sickle –
an opening of gut, a blunt knife-tip, a
forty-five-degree angle, mouth to anus
– the innards opening to a mastery
of living-room space – watching on,
a razz of witless nannies, parting
curtains, a blunt descaling, fluffing
pillows, dusting at corners, in lieu of a
tight intestinal grip, the kids – known
as claret bubs, or thingamabobs, even
toy-box swindlers chewing at the
poultry, each spooling as meretricious
glints, serenading the kitchen tiles
a gnawing
of a bouillabaisse
with their mouths wide open, teeth
wove of chopped fennel, remnants
of black sea pooling at their chins.

THINNING CUTS

i.   The dead man in the garden, the paedophile.

Heeding [**plag**] excavated pieces of meat overgrown with grass
and rotting flesh, two eyes
a cut-out sod against cloth, a rag placed over the mouth of a man.
Scalp left as roof top
coverings, laid onto bare earth set now as presentable lawn.
Elderly neighbour
eyes teeth [**giar**] castrating her own trees so as they haunt
similarly
to those in opposed garden: trimmed, pruned, slit and sheared
back, dissected and hacked as bones, clipped, incised then
carved, slashed, severed so as her own thistle bleeds.
the same demonstrable stare. Picking up teeth
woman [**iz-əm**] squishes her theories into
grape, replacing embryo with ivory
severs, or seeds of destruction–
removing small diameters
conscientiously, rapt
without shock or
interruption
upon the
lawn.

AZOIC

I
retch
on delight a
viscid spool
a
cast-
iron archive | sprang up
annals
a
lin-
eage | a
tribe of
skint men an
augur at
elbows | toothless
folk | an empty
house
        a
fam-
ished farm | malnourished
neats
                a
lamb ebbs
a
purge of
stale blood parts
a
bleating

heart | two soured eyes
milk less lips guard
    a
languid tongue |
a desert | no lakes

a

    gaping hoax
a
disease
an ephialtes of
salt-
rid basins.

I slit two lines in pursuit | each
ear, ribboning the mastoid, tiny
bows in hopes of silence, in
hopes of gills | the lining of lung
equipt to handle air, not angst | I
submerge, frogbit | teeth marks
on my wrists, air but vacuum
| solace in hypoxia, starved of
oxygen, soundless altercations |
spilt milk, split lips, black eyes;
thrips, amphipods slewing algal
fronds, gnawing through tears |
active swimmers, propelled by
hope, antennae, three pairs of
abdominal appendages |

PATHOLOGICAL LIAR

a   strato-   spheric

facade of

        cotton   candy
        that

intrudes my

                                    lips

        as   atoms, or
volent

    species,

affixing to

                              esophagi
          as
treason,

      oozing

                        past

        the

pharynx

and

guile-

fully

fattening

the eyes

of

those

keen to

devour

a

tart,

uncere-

moniou

s

scatter-

ing

of

poppy

cock,

a drivel

that

coins

in

prevol-

ence, a

a burst

of

cations   ferocious-

ly

sweet in   the

lungs.

MAUDLIN

To sit at this table is to sit in a

chamber lined of iron

spokes, the silence impaling

each one of us-

its maudlin face a

lachrymose, a wide-mouthed

sarcophagi of which opens at

the gut, we

reach inside with our tiny

hands and bleed over

the course of several hours as

to penetrate our minds

on the tip of a jovial skewer,

loosing ourselves

in a street of a thousand

jackhammers

like Tilda Swinton in

We Need to Talk

About Kevin.

OO-BLEE-ETT

I'd forget me too. I see how you think
up ways to let slip whilst reading news
bulletins of lost people found in river
beds, ankles cleft bound by silver
tongued covenants. you are
a synonymist,
lay in your chair as though buoy
ant, set along the Pasig
with your mouth
strewn together
by tiny sutures. please do,
you think, sound it out. oo-blee-
ett. ou-bli-ette. open a hatch
to the narrowest passage,
set along the farthest part
of my conscience,
shin down the unlit ex
it, tilt back your head to see
me as iron grate, knelt in your fruit
less want. and I do so at the drop
of a hat as I sip
cold tea with cart
loads of decorum
transported crab
wise, distal for perhaps eight
or so years, knowing
others may have been held
here at some point, pinching
their way out of servitude,
tissue marred by a moonless keel.

WATERING CAN

or *PARADIGMATIC TORTURE TECHNIQUES FOR KIDS WITH INCARCERATED PARENTS*

            nothing
came of it- a
sherbet
        dip, that's
what Ma coined
        it, skint-
dipping in
        and out
the 'owse
        old for
months on end,
        the
ending a
continuum-
        a bird,
each
        week a
plume
        of bruised
knuckles,
        chipped
lips- our 'eds
        strapped
to sloping
        boards,
cov
        ered
mouths of wet
        rags

brimmed with
opt

        im

        is
        m-
   dark
antrum's, a
faucet-
   our hopes
hallucinatory-
    disembog
ued,
   as though
   a
watering can
trickled
   over our
   faces
   four or
five times
   a day,
seedlings-
asphyx
   i   a
     ting
   our way
   though

     the
asphalt.

SARDINES
or *ON THE BUS, VISITING DA AT HMP FOREST BANK*

Bus skittles bones
-kegling zips-
nine-pin jostles
P
I
P
alas
tiny p

  pi
  pil
  pilc
  pilch
  pilcha
  pilchar
  pilchard
atop
harried
narrow rafts
that swamp
the archipelagos
of a quaint
tin-can.

POWDERED MILK

It is night and i am still al
ive much to the dismay of moth

er though i am bust
ling of bacteria a form

ation of plaques a coales
cence of fungi a strain of dem

ise a lost pill a contracept
ive hiccup boked and left to dis

solve an empty Lambert and But
ler packet a clomp of white clot

ting a cenotaph a commem
oration an assemblage of

innominate drifters ascribed
to inappropriate storage.

At thirty I found myself in Tillamook with a two point two five-kilogram tub of pick a mix, a lemon mosquito bite Slurpee, sandwiched between two rented cars and the Wilson River, a motel room, Arrested Development, high volume, begging the prostitute I'd paid one-hundred-and-seventy-five-dollars to fuck my boyfriend a little 'arder as to shut 'im up. choke him, i said – i'm tryin' to watch tele 'ere – do somethin', anything. right you are, he said – and he did so with a curtain tassel, a faux leather belt and as I ripped the saccharine yoke of a candied egg with my two-front teeth. I then watched the episode where Michael asks Gob's Hot Cops stripper friends to impersonate real police officers, wry outward church giggles; the hoarseness quieting with broken blood vessels, protruding eyes, ecchymosis; thick, bulbous veins as he came in my peripheral.

CUNT

I accidentally called my mother cunt
one morning as she tied my shoelaces
before nursery. I wasn't sure of its
meaning; she hadn't smiled in time
– and at that time it was an accident.
At seven, I had confused the term
with endearment – perhaps it was a
nickname supplied by Da: Where's my
dinner, cunt? Did you meet that cunt at
AA? What did you get your cunting self-
pregnant for? So- as I felt *cunt* stomping
down my bantling tongue, a harsh
cuffing of elbows in performance of the
Tungurahua – an act of kicking teeth,
a uvula trapeze that turned my cheeks
indigo – Taringa Whakarongooooo!
chimed the inner lobes of my ardent
ears with its tiny hands slewing through
my sinless lips, propelling into her face,
asphyxiating each corner of the longue.

SURRENDER

                          The
                    last push
              had me nurse
my mouth   in the
par
king lot-   rid
my tongue
                    of righteousness
              in a rear view
mirror   a bin a curb
              side of plump fats
of lip
                    for the first
time post
                    pur
                              chase
the air
              sped in vast
                    pleats that ensnared
                              at my

              gullet
a pain
wrought as
              an index ran
              along the rubber
spokes my tips
an atlas

of black tracks
             the exact moment
             of birth crawled
into my mouth
the way
a bird
circumnavigates
the wings
             of a plane   left
me
knee   capped
a panting   wreck

                    age.

to be a rat, I'm told, is to be
several things.
  I
wouldn't care to rat
on you if you were to do something
shit,
      I ain't that
arsed 'bout it truth be told, though –
you must be warned,
      I
have been likened to a rat since
infancy,
as far as rats go,
that is.
      I felt,
      since inception,
the fire, the bucket, held firmly
  upon
      my mother's back.
I
clawed my way through her ribs, her
stomach,
she

          never forgot
          it.

CHUDDY

Ma compared my Da to the surviving dregs of a half-consumed chewie, the fortuitous slice swimming the abdomen of a ten-year-old truant – Da, in Ma's eyes, slept immured, punctured, solus – weathered a-top a red-cigarette-bud-necropolis. Contemplating my father, i press a half-bit claw-like fingernail straight through the comatose, and whilst mostly unmalleable – the middle soft

> and warm and
> forgiving and
> as Ma squawks
> *GET*
> *YOUR*
> *FUCKING*
> *FINGER*
> *AWAY*
> *FROM*
> *THA*
> *RANK*
> *OLD*
> *CHUDDY*

she yanks my chassis with ease with FURY – with this a defiant trail of pepper mint fighting the strong, lippy Cumbrian winds.

PTERYGOID WALK

i.   At ten.
ii.   In conversation.
iii.   The other boy at the prison.

i can devour a
gator no pickle /
break with my arms
and legs so limb
less / heed how i hoick
my tongue ayont
the low
lands / note how i skulk
the trees coiling till
ows / infrared gog
gles / sound wave vibrat
ions / low-light recept
ors / olfactory
chambers / odor part
icles / a vacuum
ing rib cage of a
third beating lung al
        ong the trachea
waiting impatient
ly for the precise
moment to a
    m
       b
          u
   s
      h

WRONG'UN

I'd rather not talk.
Though when
asked of
how a
charbroiled mind
came to atlas,
as a
memorandum
of scar tissue, i
speak as though a
child
cooked over an
open pit
with an apple
wedged
between
my cicatrice
mouth,
as if torn
              lips
are a
good thing,
stuck with
wrists tied ayont a
molten back
roads looped out
of sight and limbs
fixt to

a rotary spit,
the tightening of
rope gives
a jaundiced map,
a scorched
coagulation of
thoughts
purged onto
the same
        boat.

EXPIRY DATE

When they found me i was dead or
ailing or lost atop a beach

less hammock straight up somersault
ing an upward vortex a choke

hold a gasp a monopoly
of clutching time, a trivial

cinch a perturbed nihility
whilst cradling that of an empty

coup an endocarp a house of
no door a husk of spilt nectar

a tang of spite a militant
sip that commands the attention

of good posture: *look* left, *look* right
a valiant pulp that blurs the

nous riding a wave so fucking
high it foams in turbulence with

its pooling sharks poised all set to
consume those steeping an up-right

departure lounge.

a chest tightness it wasn't sex, nor
food i could not call it nothing
nourished me as it should my belt
tight at my waist ground cut high
as an act of love to mess with you,
notch to prong the farthest hole

a hollow place dug into something
missed terribly serious, make babies
said your mother asked of me to
sit in your mouth, like an estuary
and take huge gulps of air was
dry strapped harshly to your face

it, with a pinch of salt marsh ooze
under quiet hums as i watch on
the television two people fuck hard
to call it love when we do this,
chain smoke cigarettes for break-
fast speed boat along a riverbed.

DARK, HIGHLY SATURATED

to know
me is to drill
diligently
into the earths
crust, a steel
lubricated tip-
sit, await
the mantle-
it takes
perhaps nine-
teen years
to do so, be
sure to weld
shut after
wards.

i see mother break
down yeast
by psalm

to a
mid golden
loaf seedless rye.
i see mother
act

out

the brokenness

of her body-

tooth rind

tear apart
tangy
taste satsuma.
i see mother blade
tip slice seeds

a

quartering
tomato spilling out
counter-top
bulbs

                    of garlic
                spread spores

                water batter
flour knead,

                i see toe
            nail fungus dead
                cord grass worn
                    by barefoot
bones house
                        floors

                streaked bacon
    skulls,   i see
                all the above,
                    tottering

beneath her.

HIDDEN

a door veiled by war
drobe of old covers
stink like sour rhubarb

    rupture a dark lodge
    ment, an upward route
    stairwell talk about

        a white faience sink
        drip rust pustules
        upon prying tongues.

ACKNOWLEDGEMENTS

Thank you to Dr. Wendy Vaizey of Kingston University for kindly taking a chance on me back in 2021. I developed a handful of these poems whilst under the tuition of some great teachers at Kingston. To my fellow students at Kingston, thanks for your patience of my participation on screen perched at the end of a table, greatly appreciated. Special gratitude to Terry Craven and the team at Desperate Literature for shortlisting my short story, "Surströmming." I shall never forget how incredible you all were, and how fulfilling the experience was to be featured in your anthology- Eleven Stories. Editor Jess Chandler, a huge thank you for selecting my piece to be published in Prototype. Ottessa Moshfegh for her kind words, support and much needed encouragement post MFA. Gregory McCartney and Susanna Galbraith of Abridged Magazine. Writers Mallory Smart, Tiffany Michelle Brown. To my parents, and Joseph- I love you always. Finally, Aaron Kent, and everyone at Broken Sleep for allowing me to publish my first pamphlet.

I am forever indebted to you all.

LAY OUT YOUR UNREST